CW00944033

ANCHOR BOOKS

INSPIRATIONS FROM THE SOUTH 2002

Edited by

Katie Coles

First published in Great Britain in 2002 by
ANCHOR BOOKS
Remus House,
Coltsfoot Drive,
Peterborough, PE2 9JX
Telephone (01733) 898102

All Rights Reserved

Copyright Contributors 2002

HB ISBN 1 85930 932 1
SB ISBN 1 85930 937 2

FOREWORD

Anchor Books is a small press, established in 1992, with the aim of promoting readable poetry to as wide an audience as possible.

We hope to establish an outlet for writers of poetry who may have struggled to see their work in print.

The poems presented here have been selected from many entries. Editing proved to be a difficult task and as the Editor, the final selection was mine.

I trust this selection will delight and please the authors and all those who enjoy reading poetry.

Katie Coles
Editor

CONTENTS

WHAT I WANT

A world full of peace,
And pockets full of money,
A big house filled with rooms,
With the weather always sunny.

Equality for woman and man,
No more rich or poor,
A classless society,
A life worth living for.

Good health for all around,
A life filled with laughter,
The love of a good man,
To live happy ever after.

A good education for my children,
For their wishes to come true,
This is what I want
How about you?

Sharon Brehaut

MOUSETRAP

There's a mouse in the attic scratching about
I hear it whilst lying in bed.
Up amongst the old books, and furniture store
and a huge spider spinning its web.

I wonder how he got up in the attic above
p'raps by magic, I'm sure it must be.
Or up through the pipes, he climbed to the top
to live there in safety, you see.

I wonder how long he thinks he'll survive
up there with no food, only dust.
An' that spider watching from up there above
thinking that mouse for dinner's a must.

Tomorrow, I'll trap him with a big chunk of cheese
but his scratches keeps me from sleep?
I'll quieten him down, I'll set the trap now
whilst he scratches my treasures I keep.

He'll sniff at the cheese with his long thin snout
you'll hear a scurry, and then not a peep.
Then a crack, then a squeak, that's the end of the noise
of that scratching that keeps me from sleep.

Pat Thoume

SHOPPING LIST

Squeezed to a stoop behind smoked glass,
Sister Margaret Mary
the oldest nun.

She kneels in front of me,
incense around; we are at morning Mass
in the little chapel.

The rose garden's in slats
and Latin drips.

Countdown's in swirl, I see her
freshmint in silk-lined oak, stoop gone,
straight as dignity.

Respectfully,
I make a mental note
to replace the toothpaste.

Patricia Maubec

VILLAGE AFFAIRS

So the time of year has come again
When timid ladies act like men.
Their muscles bulge, they kick and spit
With villagers shocked at every hit.
'Gather 'round the green tonight
To watch the annual ladies' fight.'
People come, it's a compulsory thing,
Booing and cheering around the ring:
'Come on, we know you'll do us proud'
(And all of this depending on how
The public perceives each woman to be,
Good for nothing, or a sweet lady.)
But what I think is most surprising,
Is the reason for this fighting -
Shouldn't they just have a private debate
To decide who will host the village fête?

Anna Brehaut

GUERNSEY

Of gull grey, dull grey, glittering granite
The habitat of cormorant, guillemot and gannet.
Sea waves crash and sea spray splash,
Where Guernsey clad, Guernsey lads dash.

Picture then, the fishermen, in broad beamed boats,
With winches and nets and bobbers and ropes.
Pots in trots and rollock and anchor,
All combined to fish Pollock and chancre.

A grand man, the land man, ploughing the soil,
Hoeing and sowing and growing his toil.
Fenceless field, the common ground,
With cattle grazing rights, profound.

In privateer and pirate years, long past,
The ecological mould was cast.
The seigneur shrewd, the feudal mule,
For centuries did his fiefdom rule.

Smooth yellow sand, green mellow land,
Where houses and history and heritage stand.
French by connection, British by election,
A community committed to right protection.

James Willis

SOMEONE DID LIVE THERE

The house was left abandoned
   In need of great repair
The sound of voices quiet now
   Yes someone did live there
Curtains framed the windows and
   Carpet covered stairs
Toys lay in the hallway and
   Families sat on chairs
The garden lawn was neatly mowed
   Flowers and shrubs were springing
In the corner standing tall
   The children's swing was swinging
Yes someone did live there
   The cat in the porch all warm and purring
Waiting for the family's return
   She would greet them with a friendly wail
A nudge from her head and a flick from her tail
   Yes someone did live there

Sue Marquand

THAMES PATH

Cormorants drying wings outstretched,
Puddle ducks with young,
Flitting seagulls, doves or pigeons
In the shifting, shimmering exit tide.

Ring doves and magpies, geese and heron,
Raven and mallard, walking and swimming,
Nesting and mating.

Low water Thames as washing line,
Trees reflecting upside down
Sluices and houseboat jetties,
Ship ways and dingies,
Storm water outlets fifty metres from here.

Dog walkers and cyclists, rowers and waders
Share my aloneness, runners and joggers
Heart and lungs pounding, heels and knees contacting
Earth, grass and pebbles.

This is our right of way
Need of way, hideaway.
Wood smoke and ozone
Perspiration and seaweed
Alternately blending.

Cawing and calling, lapping and humming,
Rumbling and roaring, shrieking and moaning,
Mumbling and panting
The river flows on.

Christine E Rowe

BUNDLE

Semblance of refuse-bag
outside the doorway you sit,
Curled - huddled - dot-like
punctuating - full stop
space.
While silence spells out
Help! – Homeless! - Helpless!

Waves of humanity trampling
unseeing
near stumbling in the rush,
Dart thought-arrows cutting
the air.
'Get a job!' 'Druggy!' 'Council help?'
'Lay-about!'
'It's so thin!' 'Poor thing!'
'Are you genuine?' 'Are you false?'
'Oh! smell!' 'Can't tell!'
'Move on!'
Skipping young child towards
The 'Dot'.

'Can I? - can I - put something
in the pot?'

Sringkhala

FEELINGS

I feel, therefore I am.
Isn't that what Descartes said?

Feelings;
they are best buried! Or are they?

We try to submerge pain
Won't let it come up.
Feelings;
They are best buried?

She says she doesn't love me,
I don't care; but I do!
Feelings;
they are best buried.

He says, he wishes he were dead.
Why tell me?
Feelings;
they are best buried.

I don't want to know,
don't put your thoughts into my head.
Feelings;
they are best buried.

I think, therefore I am.
That's what he said.

Thinking is worse!

Jean Washbourne

TO FLEUR

There's none so lovely as our Fleur,
There's none so gorgeous as her.
I adore her and ever shall,
A captive, she holds me in thrall.

Alas, I very much fear
Her affections are elsewhere.
Still she reigns o'er me like a queen:
The nicest lady I've never seen.

But the camera cannot lie
So I'll love her till I die.

Gordon E Gompers

FIRA, THE SEA LAWYER FOR SATIRE

I think I saw a unicorn, with a mane and tail of fire.
It reared up high, then flew into the sky;
Higher and higher.
This creature so fine and fair, was mine to admire!

It flew with a lady unpon it;
Who was blessed with fine attire
Playing on a small lyre!
Surely this was a sight, for any soul to aspire!

I watched as this finely groomed creature
Then danced upon a quicksilver wire
Adorned with diamonds and rubies,
Emeralds and a sapphire.

I thought of how this creature,
I could then acquire
As it emerged from the Atlantic Ocean,
From a diamond castle in Eire.

Sparks arose from its hooves
As it rode still higher and higher
Before the ocean roared,
Like a great lion guarding its empire.

But then it seemed to me,
Knowing regard of what would transpire -
Was that this unicorn was actually my spirit:
Whom I then named 'Desire'.

Colette Breeze

MOVING CLOUD

Moving cloud like solemn creatures
  Passing to reveal
A flower blue where light is
  Root of its appeal.

Barnaby Thornton Lockyer

ROSEMARY

Did you think you could just leave me
And everything would be OK?
Did you think I would find another
To love and share my life?

No, I cannot blame you
You had no choice in things
The Angel of death came merciful
And carried your soul away.

I have prayed for your return
Or to let me go to you
I only know I cannot, with any worth
Live life without your love.

The house is now my dark fortress
Strong the love that chains me to your shrine
What hand of fate could be so cruel?
What punishment or deed does fit this crime?

The birds, they sing sweet as ever
But they touch no chord with me
The evening sun lights up the heavens
Though my eyes let in no joy.

Food is just a fuel now, for politeness
I feign appreciation and taste
For the hand that prepared my food with love
Another dish will never grace.

I know you want me, for the children,
To be strong
God give me strength, let me find the light
That shone from her beautiful heart.

Roy Baker

FAIRY RING

The smile hiding the fear marks the end
I never asked for the till receipt and I regret that now
As the goblins emerge from their holes, I see my foolishness
I gave away my gifts and saw denial thereafter for my efforts
Who'd have thought it with eyes so big and wide and soft?
I'll surprise you yet when the cold moon climbs into the sky one night
And you find yourself crumbling, ageing and worn
I'll be there. I always am.

Andy Hinkinson-Hodnett

CHERRY ORCHARD

Another spring
And cherry blossom
Clusters
Like ballet dancers
Along the branch:
Enchanting the eye.

Another week
And the dancers
Wither
Like old skin
On the grass:
Breaking the heart.

Jill Truman

SEEN FROM A TRAIN

A white blizzard
Needling the skin
Horizontally

In the corner of the white cemetery
By the angel of death
Six black figures
Curving
Six black umbrellas
Shielding
Their faces from hail and grief
Surrounding
The black hole

Patterning
The white earth
Six red wreaths
Like blood
Spilling

Jean Medcalf

YOUNG LONE SAILOR

One day a young lone sailor
Came drifting home from the sea
He met a young lone maiden
In love they came to be
But time would tell a story
Of broken dreams and tears
For as with all lone sailors
He'd sail away for years
For he needs to travel
He needs to ride
He's only really happy
When the stars they are his guide
He needs to wander
Far across the sea
He's had to stop pretending
His love could ever be
Now the sailor sailed for many years
Then once more came back home
The maiden was still waiting
Much older she had grown
She put this question to him
'Please will you leave the sea?'
But the sailor quickly answered
'My love that cannot be
For I need to travel I need to ride
I'm only really happy when the stars they are my guide
I need to wander far across the sea
I've had to stop pretending our love could ever be.'

John Wayre

DAUGHTER OF THE MORNING STAR: PART THREE

I once met a girl
As beautiful as the rain
Her laughter echoed in my ears
As that of a thousand faeries
Her touch as soft as love itself
She was my angel.

I remember the night she gave me her trust
And cried in my arms
I remember our first kiss
A surprise in the darkness
We drank so much that night
I remember the fear
The uncertainty that came with it all.

Then we drifted
For a short time
But long enough
To take my angel into the arms of another
The bitter truth is
I lost my princess
I was found by my very own prince
And she by hers.

Now we are older
I want to feel the fear again
The uncertainty
The dizziness of it all
In the tumult of my youth
I chose the wrong path
Now I shall never know
If my angel would have answered my call
If only I had asked the question.

Ali Forward-Preedy

ENGLAND 2002

Castles nestling in green and ancient hills
Blessed and hallowed turf and beautiful summer days
where noble men stand proud in all their glory.
This is a land for kings and for queens.
My land, my home, a place to never feel alone.
Albion rests gently here within earth's centre
Rich green land cradling me comfortingly, my saviour and my truth
A sacred country, very essence of these bones.

Jan Tozer

GLASTONBURY CHRISTMAS

The Glastonbury Thorn stands stark and bare
Upon a mound of green, outside a city wall,
Recalling to the troubled Christian gaze
Another naked tree and time and place.

The Glastonbury Thorn at Christmastide,
Huddles amongst the conflict of its spikes
Buds, like the fingers of the Infant Christ, which twine
Heedless, among the crown of thorns, whose petals shine
Like newborn faces in a spiteful world.

The Glastonbury Thorn's soft scent and flower
Spring from the roots which reach to the ancient well
Until the petalled Babe among the boughs
Is suckled from the source of life which flows
Freely beneath the green of Calvary,
Offering in winter's death the secret of new life.

The tree, the thorns, the flower and the hill,
The sacred spring, which rises but to heal,
Bring to the spirit Christ's rebirth once more,
Our finite rock yields ever to death's flaw
Through which is forced, infinite and unchecked,
The source of all our being
Golgotha stands defeated by a child
And hell itself is quenched beneath the sacred spring.

E C King

WANT OF THOUGHT

In bars, discos, clubs, with pick-ups many,
I failed to take precautions with any.

Exchanges of pleasure when in good health
Lulled suspicions of contagion by stealth.

Unthinking we failed to use common sense
When deciding with caution to dispense,

No word was spoken, nor a suggestion
One might be carrying a grave infection -

What had been passed on was the virus AIDS,
I knew once stricken by it all hope fades -

It simply becomes a matter of time
Before one sinks into final decline -

Too much carousing, the wine, sex, and song
With many partners was unwise and wrong,

How many there were is beyond my ken,
Blame surely resting on how we lived then,

Convinced now if I'd behaved differently
I'd have avoided what's happened to me.

Laura Edwards

BEYOND THE LAND OF THE MISERY GUTS

The more worldy
the less narrow and silly
I hope I've become.
For to spend one's days
wearing the grey death mask
of another's stupid misery
is to live amongst the shadows,
in some place between
life and death.

And if it wasn't for the fences we build
from the condescending voices
of doubt and discouragement,
it would be just you and me;
our footsteps briefly carved
into a deserted shore,
as we wait to ride
upon the white horses
of the morning tide.

For the journeys I take
and the friendships I make
are all special ones,
special to me.

Michael Wilson

A WOMAN BELOW

In olden days. Above high on a cross,
Among criminals, Oh! What a loss.
It was an ugly sight to see.
Onlookers looked in rhapsody.

Asphyxiated, due to the heat and stench
A woman below whose heart did wrench.
Why weepiest woman? Can you not see!
This is what the prophets said would be.

The heavens, and glory did hold!
High went the spirit, leaving the body cold.
Mourners all around did see.
A spirit floating in tranquillity.

Ann Hubbard

No Muse Is Bad Muse

Your letter fell upon my mat,
I read it through and sighed, 'That's that,'
My Muse has flown, just like a bird,
And left me wordless, with no word.

I coaxed, cajoled, I did my best,
I fought, I flirted, beat my chest,
But not a jot, a jape or jest . . .
My Muse had gone, had flown the nest.

No jingle, ditty, clerihew,
No rondeau, couplet or haiku,
No sonnet, stanza, villanelle,
No nursery rhyme, no ding dong bell.

'Any subject,' you have said,
There *are* no subjects in my head,
No ship of dreams to climb aboard,
To help me win your cash award.

My Muse is like the boomerang
That Charlie Drake bemoaned and sang,
'It won't come back,' he vocalised,
So here am I . . . de-rhymeatised.

Meanwhile I hope you'll keep in touch,
And send a straw for me to clutch,
For though I live, theoretically,
I'm quite, quite dead, poetically.

Audrey Loftin

LONDON - 5TH APRIL 2002

Brilliant sunshine, freezing wind, flags at half mast,
Crowds already here waiting to see the possession go past,
It took hundreds of people all night,
To clear the way so everyone might,
See the Queen Mother's coffin pass slowly down,
On a gun carriage covered with her colours and crown,
The Queen Mother's last salute to the nation,
Her family on foot behind, regardless of station,
Being taken to Westminster Abbey to lie in state,
Where thousands will pass at a slow rate,
She was well past a hundred and one,
That is why most people have come.
Whatever happened she was always there,
It did not matter when or where,
As they pass drum beats to give right pace,
She is not leaving a gap more a space.
When you speak to people here whatever their race,
They all say there will never be anybody to take her place.

Florence Macleod

GOD'S STORY

To wander in the countryside and see,
The oak, the elm and ash,
Watch the lambs within fields so green
Cutting such a dash.

To see so many colours true,
Orange, yellow, red and blue.
Buttercups, daisies, roses, violets too,
The colour of the leaves on trees,
And the buzzing of the bees.

The song of birds upon the wing,
And all around at peace and ease,
The love and peace, the toil and labour,
And how to: really love our neighbour.

Add the sun to all this glory
To make up God's most wondrous story.

Gordon E Miles

WAKEHURST GARDEN

The lovely garden, linked to Kew
Is at its best in early spring,
With daffodils that bloom again,
And blossom-laden shrubs in view.

The tranquil lake reflects it all,
The stately building in the sun,
The carefully tended patio,
With lots of seats for everyone.

The nesting season for the birds
Who fill the morning air with song,
The rhododendrons' early buds
Promise their glory won't be long.

So sit and dream amidst the charm
Of nature's beauty at its best
And marvel at the loveliness,
That all around is manifest.

Leonard T Coleman

A NEW DAY RISING

A glimmer of orange
A highlight of hope
Sun's orb arising
Shining out with such warmth.
Birds all a-flutter feed off the land
Rabbits are grooming
Or digging in sand.
Raptors fly highest,
Mewling, such calls!
Soaring the South Downs
High o'er farmland walls.
And higher as it rises, spreading
Sunshine across the sea
Seabirds, flocking, feeding,
Feasting on fishy weed.
Waders in the shallows hunt and peck
Herons espy fishes
And stab when in the mood.
Crabs crawl sideways, hiding
Out in the slimy mud,
And higher, spreading evenly
The sunrays like some flood.
Shedding, flowing life-light
Hot, so golden round
One feels it on an antler,
Strange, it makes no sound.

Martha Watson Brown

THE KIMBERLY DUNNY

There's a little green tin dunny
In the north of Kimberly
Where the outback is as rough as it can get
Where the roads are corrugated
And the dirt's Australian red
And you just don't try to drive there in the wet.

As you climb the steps outside it
To the ease we all must seek
You can sit and read the notice on the wall
It's environmentally friendly
Just rots itself away
And Brownie comes to clean it once a week.

It may not be a palace
Just a small and shabby hut
But just remember this when you set forth
When you see it in the distance
As it stands above the trees
It's a welcome sight to all us blokes up north.

Don B Harper

THE COUNTY OF KENT

To me the county of Kent is the best in the land
In the south eastern corner surrounded by sand
The North Sea to the east, the English Channel to the south
And the Isle of Sheppey at Medway's mouth
There's Dreamland at Margate, a place to have fun
Also other places of interest second to none
Places like Leed's castle and Penshurst Place
And the White Cliffs of Dover with its chalky face
The birds sheltering in the safety of Pegwell Bay
And Canterbury Cathedral, what more can I say?
Reculver Towers and the farmland with crops abound
And the sound of the waves crashing all around.

Then there's the Pantiles in Royal Tunbridge Wells
The taking of the spring waters any sickness it quells.
The steam train that runs through the Kent countryside
Through Romney, Hythe and Dymchurch you can go for a ride
There's Chartwell, Winston Churchill's grand abode
And Chatham Dockyard, where history of the Navy is shown
Hever Castle, the ruins of Bodium and Knole House
And Chilham Castle where they ride horses and joust.
North Foreland Lighthouse that saved sailors from being drowned
The Goodwin Sands where many a ship has gone to ground.
There's the Whitbread Farm at Beltring and many more
Which is why I'll always live in Kent, the county I adore.

Celia Law

TELL ME IT'S NOT TRUE!

A Sheppey postman was heard to say
It's rumoured I'm being posted right away,
Covering Sittingbourne and Milton Creek,
In the winter the future's very bleak.
Every morning, our bridge is probably up
I honestly feel I've been 'sold a pup',
Going to miss going home to a lovely lunch
I'll end up surviving on a McDonald's brunch.
Miss calls to that widow on Bat and Ball Hill,
I fancy her rotten, she really gives me a thrill,
I'd deliver a parcel to her without any fee,
Hope it's not long before she invites me for tea.
Keep it to yourself please, don't tell my wife,
Otherwise I know she will give me some strife,
Then she will put paid to my very special treat,
She always scrubs my back on Wednesday, every week.
I've got to be firm and I'll feel a real louse,
When I tell my wife we have to sell the house,
She'll miss her yoga and dinners with the WI
Do I have to go working overseas, why oh why?
Just as I was getting accepted by Sheppey dogs,
With a brand new outfit, yes, I've got new togs.
But if they say I've to go, I'll really scream,
What a relief it is that it's only a bad dream!

Fred Grimwade

YHA ROAMING - BROMLEY

Well now my friend - where next will you roam?
First the depths of the rainforest - now Mornington near home.
With the caravan club and friends by your side,
you travel the country - far and wide.
The call of the wild - it must be said,
makes you hitch up your trailer - and with
gold sparkling earrings and a bandeau of red,
you're off!

Well now my friend, I know where to roam,
it's up to the shops - then trudge back home.
Instead of a rucksack - I'm carrying shopping
and to catch my breath - I have to keep stopping.
The call of the wild is from my old man Fred,
who tells me he's hungry and needs to be fed.
I'm off.

Jean M Eyre

TURBULENT FOAM!

Thoughts meditative search, has far to roam
Seeking an elusive poem.
Chewed pen lingers, poised over clean paper,
White, as surging sea foam.

Mind now bold, scolds inspiration
Strolling with dragging shoelaces,
Through the ebbing tide of white foam.

Floundering amongst sullen thought, to sink.
Fraught refusal to assemble,
Correct metre as told.

Stepping stones, words new penned,
Gleaming wet with ink, appear from turbulent foam.
Ideas immersed, surface to be jubilantly beachcombed,
Clasped at last, elusive poem . . . !

Joanne Manning

NEPTUNE'S KISS

(On dimly viewing Isle of Sheppey from Holly Hill Boughton)

I ache to seethe a poem
Flecked with Neptune's rays
Lines that dance in dappled shifts
Of light, that heaves and sprays.
I want to feel, full fathoms deep,
The press of southern seas,
Breasting the bows to kink my wake
While creaking mast and turgid sails
Grasp the ebb-ward breeze.

I want to etch a portrait
Scraped from the ebb and flow
Of pitch-tossed ranks of charging arcs
That hem in the bay below.
I want to see the horizon's lip
Lanced by a brown, bent sail
That bares the brunt of the ocean's clout
On a dogged bowsprit's tip.

Yet all I see is the ragged sun
Chilling the blasted beech.
Dancing the leaves past silent ewes
On a hill top's lofty breech.
While set below - full twenty leagues
The anchored isle - beset with gale,
Sheathed in marching cloud,
Lies in the lee of spindrift's rage
And melts in the dusky seas.

John P Rose

THE GREAT DIVIDE

Silhouetted against the street light,
Shoulders hunched,
Uniformly clad in jeans and trainers,
Sweatshirts.
The non-hopers.
Taking drugs, smoking, idling hours away.
No spur, no aim in life,
Motionless.

Then galvanised to life, their arms flail out,
Smashing, destroying,
Scrawling graffiti everywhere.

Is this the generation we have spawned?
Is this the generation that we want?
And yet the coin has two sides.

We see the youngsters striving hard
To make their name in sport;
They run and swim, sponsored to raise
The money for some well-deserved charity;
Digging the gardens of the elderly,
Excelling in their schools,
Achieving high results,
Making their parents and community
So proud of them.

Why the two sides?
Why the great divide?
Why have we let them down?
Where have we gone wrong?

We must take heart, not merely acquiesce,
Not turn away.
With us, the older generation, lies the task
Of building bridges 'cross the great divide.

Roma Davies

THE STRANGER AT THE DOOR

I opened my heart and love walked in and left the door ajar.
I thought my dreams had all come true and I'd caught a falling star.
Little did I know that day that when the door was open wide.
The person that I loved walked in with a stranger at his side.
The person whom I loved so much soon became my soul mate,
The stranger with whom he walked hand in hand, I began to hate.
The stranger I tried so hard to ignore and pretend he wasn't there,
But he played his own game rules, which never seemed quite fair.
Every time the stranger left I tried to close the door,
But he demanded to be let in and couldn't be ignored.
I never really knew when he'd return and demand to be let in,
But I knew he couldn't be reasoned with and he would always win.
I have wanted to accept the stranger who walks at my loved one's side,
But if my heart can't take the strain I want to say, 'I tried!'

Jackie Washington

MAY

Girl with a rice paper face
pimpernel breezes
squeeze over the fields of May
red admiral,
alphabet bits scattered all over the place
beside stones shining
like jewel sequins through bitter grasses
parting company between clouds.
Tonight a vixen laps at water
while children are sleeping in dreams
where the bull rushes part.

Graham J Fairbrass

THE QUEEN MOTHER
(In loving memory of The Queen Mother - 1900-2002)

Let the whole nation grieve,
In this time of terrible sadness,
Many may find their emotions,
Almost impossible to express.
The Queen Mother brought much to our lives,
Kindness, love, affection and joy,
She had such an amazing zest for life,
Not even the bombs of war could destroy.

Let the whole nation mourn,
A lady loved by young and old,
Who will remain in our hearts forever,
And in memories and stories told.
There will never ever be such a wonderful person,
The Queen Mother was truly one of a kind,
She will now become a saint and an angel,
Whose rays of love nothing will outshine.

Rest in eternal peace.

Robin J Grigsby

FREE SPIRIT

There are many places I want to be
For my mind to explore and my eyes to see.
Down in the valleys within the breeze;
Locked in a dream and forgotten the keys.
Over the mountains, beyond the sea,
These are the places where I feel free.
Riding on horseback through an endless field,
And crushing fierce demons with sword and shield.

Sail me around the world's great seas,
On a raft made from solid oak trees.
Sink me down in a submarine,
I will dive to depths where no man's been.
Explore the ocean floor,
To discover great treasures never seen before.

Let me fly a fighter jet,
To protect the earth beneath my wing.
Sit me on a throne,
To feel just like a king.
Put me on a shooting star,
Into space,
Who cares how far?

Ending on a journey to heaven's gate.
Though just for a peek,
My turn can wait.

Darren J Abbott

TO KOS - JUST BECAUSE . . .

Soon I'm going away to a wonderful isle
The thought of it lights up my face with a smile
It's set in the Aegean sea, all sparkling and bright
And the more I think about it
I know it was right because . . .
A week or two of feeling free
Can make all the difference for you and for me.

Because of your beaches
Because of the sea
Because you're so sunny
Kos - you're for me!

Balmy sun-drenched beaches
How I long for you
Glinting white villas do not detract from the view
How I bathe in your beauty on grey London days
In my dreams about Kos about whom historians have raved
Over the centuries.

Because of your beaches
Because of the sea
Because you're so sunny
Kos - you're for me!

So now very soon
I will see for myself what has made lovers croon -
Castles and mosques, cafes and bars,
Discos, tavernas and shops.
Kos, don't let me down and I'll be over the moon . . .

Because of your beaches
Because of the sea
Because you're so sunny
Kos - you're for me!

Now Kos is just a memory, I'm ever so sad
It was everything we'd hoped for and more
I'd go there again at the drop of a hat
Although sadly because of plane spotters
It's now off the map of happy holiday shores
But then different countries had different 'mores'.
If they succeed in fair justice when they appeal
Britons will once again visit with zeal.

Elaine Hunt

SEGMENTING THE GRAPEFRUIT . . .
CAUTERISING THE WOUND

damn the relentless salt in its blistering undying mode
that leaves its tidemark on sorry lives, on souls and the rocky
Damascus road
poured into the gash that festers as we turn and stroll away . . .
'it's only love and love is lost' . . . I heard the poet say
damn the heart that beats its drum in this pile of mortgaged bricks
that leaves its mark in every derelict hole and every 'pump' that ticks
it finds its feet in unharvested fields and alleys where
'children' play . . .
'it's only love and love is lost' . . . I heard the poet say
damn the ash that settles when the grave is left for cold
that leaves its dust and memories in undug winter mould
it finds its way into our eyes and our icons made of clay . . .
'it's only love and love is lost' . . . I heard the poet say
damn the flesh that bears the brunt of every brutal act
that wears its scars and broken veins of every licensed pact
it ponders its fleeting moments in its last throes of decay . . .
'it's only love and love is lost' . . . I heard the poet say.

Bill Talbott

OUR CENOTAPH

Our Cenotaph means so much to us,
In Whitehall it proudly stands,
Portraying all that has gone before,
Men and women fallen in war,
Due to the magnitude of their plight,
We have freedom and the right,
To carry on living and not to fight,
Men and women march along,
Having fought in war in days gone,
So proud they are, with heads held high,
Bringing more than one tear to the eye,
Some still suffering from their wounds,
To the Cenotaph turn their heads
From all walks of life,
They did more than their best,
Medals prominent upon their chest,
Marching in time with military bands,
November weather chilling their hands,
Their heads full of memories of
Lost friends, of battles won and lost
We have freedom in this land of ours,
Just think - then count the cost,
Too often there is not enough thought,
Of these various heroes in wars fought,
We never learn from lessons taught,
With trouble and strife the world is fraught.

John H Israel

VOYAGE WITH THE JARGON-AUTS

I'm going to sign on for a management course;
I've just read an advert about it.
It seems my assertiveness rating's deficient;
And I'm destined for failure without it.

Any knowledge and skills I relied on before
Will, they say, only take me so far;
I need training in psycho-synthetics
And my self-esteem's way under par.

A diploma in modern stress-management
Will provide what my life has been lacking
And with it my shelf-filling job at the store
Will lead to promotion . . . not sacking.

So I'm travelling hopefully onward,
The course will get all my attention,
Though it's not just the leadership role that I seek,
But a great big fat pay cheque and pension.

Norman Ford

EARTH TO EARTH

There is contentment in my soul,
For all the jewels of the ancient kingdoms
Are mine, here in Gloucestershire.

The buttercup and Dymock's daffodils
Layer the springtime meadows with their gold,
With coral bird's eye speckling the grass
And bluebells' sapphire haze beneath the trees.

My pearls are scattered on the Cotswold hills,
As rounded sheep strung out across the vale
Above the bubbling streams and cameo pools
Where hunts the darting, cobalt kingfisher.

My diamonds are the droplets of a dew
Borne upon a silvered quivering web;
Live orbs of wavering, iridescent light
Set amongst the glistening ruby haws.

Across Sabina's deep carnelian flow,
Lie Dean's majestic gnarled and emerald oaks
Encircling secret pools, whose opalescent gleam
Reflect infinity beyond a topaz sky.

And I shall end my days as I began
In Gloucestershire.

Una Dowding

A Passing Thought

Life for all is transient,
Its duration is unknown.
Tragedy can strike at any time
Without a forewarning of reason or rhyme,
And hopes for the future postponed.
The greatest joys won't last forever,
So make the most of every day;
Youth and beauty time will sever,
But sincere love has no decay.

Bryan Colman Bird

Lost In The Snow

On a night of snow, in the drifting white,
A sudden flash caught my sight,
I tiptoed to the window, so I could investigate the flash,
Suddenly I heard a noise like some glass all smashed,
The snow was white like extra thick cream,
I watched the floor by the ice-filled stream,
The stream made the noise because it smashed
But the trouble was, what was the flash?
I went downstairs and put on my clothes
I got outside and everything was froze,
Hooray, hooray, I know the flash
It was a lovely star in a dash.
I followed the star and bumped into a tree
I fell over and grazed my knee
I looked around but there was just white,
My house was not in sight.
I called for help but nobody came,
I was all alone, what a shame.
A piece of grass crawled off a twig
It crawled to the floor and began to dig.
Sorry, I'm mistaken, it wasn't a twig
It was a stick insect that began to dig
He scuttled on my shoulder and began to talk
'Dig this tunnel, it's where you'll walk.'
So it was a tunnel he dug, silly old me.
Where will it take me? We will see.
The tunnel was finished and he let me in
I walked in and said goodbye to him.
I walked and walked until it finally stopped
I pushed the top and out I popped
I knew where I was when I saw a door,
I was on my bedroom floor.

Ashley Robertson (7)

A MOTHER'S LIFE, MY LIFE

I could have been a mother of seven,
But Jesus gently took two to heaven.
Life is very hard even with five,
But the love I have is worth the strive.

I sometimes sit and wonder why?
Where I've gone wrong and then I cry.
You see I'm a wife as well as a mother,
But there is no love for one another.

Bit by bit my feelings went,
The abuse and blows my husband sent.
Life is so short, this is not fair,
But he does not think, nor does he care.

My children are fifteen years down to three,
That's why I must stay, do you see?
Tomorrow brings another day
Good or bad, who can say?

A mother and wife I will still be,
Until Jesus above hands me the key.
Then I will be reunited as a mother of seven
In a peaceful place, my home, my heaven.

Sharon Freeman

YOU

You are the man I love
Your embrace fits like a glove.

Your smile brightens my day
Your feet show me the way.

You are my best friend
I will be with you till the end.

Your touch is gentle and rough
Of you, I can't get enough.

You are the father of my children
I would surely do it all again.

You are beautiful, handsome and smart
You have completely stolen my heart.

You are kind, generous and sensitive
You give me a reason to live.

You and your love give me confidence
Living now all makes sense.

You support me in all that I do
I want to be with no one but you.

Without you I am but half a person
I love you, again and again.

Joanne M Brown

THE SEA

The sea was beautiful today,
Sunlight sparkled like jewels in the glistening spray,
The mermaids could be heard far, far away,
Their haunting voices filled the air,
As dolphins swam together in pairs.

Fishermen's nets went into the sea,
Catching the fish that were wild and free.
No clouds could be seen in the velvet sky,
Only the seagull's lonely cry could be heard above the crested waves,
Rolling gently into open caves.

Wendy Sims

My Window Reflection

Through my window I sit, tonight I'm alone.
From the radio that plays a song called
'My Hometown', for a moment in time it
Reminds me of back home, as tonight
I'm here in Brecon.
Looking out of my window, seeing valleys
As the evening draws in, the mountains I see
Not too far in the distance of cloud-covered peaks
That fade to the eye of the forest I see
Before me now of colours green to brown,
This forest that could hold so many secrets
But what they hold we'll never know.
As the thin blue sky's soon to turn to night,
As I stare into these clouds of the night, on a
Journey to where we'll never know.
Through my window tonight I see before me
A mirror reflection of myself but still I see right
Through myself, like that of a ghost of the night.
As this world today turns from day to night, will
Clouds break free to reveal the stars and moon,
And will the morning call out of the early bird to
Bring me the colours once again of God's green earth?

Craig Alan Hornby

TO BE A WRITER

It's grand to be a writer
It carries so much weight
That if you're absent-minded
It will exonerate.

It's neat to be a writer
Get all your words in line
Entrance the folk with music
Bring treasure from the mine.

It's fun to be a writer
Completely at your ease
While aiming friendly fireworks
At those you love to tease.

It's cool to be a writer
I think that's what you say
Since 'brill' and 'fab' and 'magic'
Are surely quite passé

It's good to be a writer
To hear the heavens call
Stew up the words with anguish
Then spill the beans to all

It's odd to be a writer
Like a virgin giving birth
Friends hail the Child as mighty
Yet wonder: how on earth?

It's time to be a writer
(One hoping to be read)
Without release from sentence
Till heart and brain are dead.

Richard Tapley

WE THREW OUR BABIES

We threw our babies to the sky.
We threw them high.
And when they tumbled
Sure into our arms
With breathless more
We threw them higher than before.

Pamela Gardner

THEY COOK, WE COOK, DO COOK. PLEASE COOK

We go on holidays abroad and
get the tastebuds for their food,
Whatever happened to bangers and mash,
jellied eels and corned beef hash?

Out British beef with Yorkshire pud,
Fish and chips that taste so good.
Steak pie with mushy peas,
Let's keep traditional meals please.

Everyone seems to plump for an Indian,
Chinese, French and also Italian.
The USA, not to be outdone,
Have us eating burgers in a bun.

Hot dogs, popcorn, we munch at the flicks,
It's a wonder we're not all permanently sick.

Enjoy these foods to eat as you will,
But let's keep British the top of the bill.

Enid Thomas

APRIL TIME

The sun is shining oh so bright
Filling the day with its wondrous light
But the wind is really quite chill
Even though it's almost mid April
Daffodils and tulips abound
Green shoots are appearing from deep underground
Birds are singing their joyful song
To tell us summer won't be very long.
They let us know that spring is here
A gentle, yet special time of the year.

June M Peek

HEARTSTRINGS

On days like this, when skies are blue,
I look up to the Heavens and think of you,
Because somewhere in this world there must be
A special place for just you and me.

I would follow any star
And climb a mountain to find where you are,
Battle my way through a tempestuous storm,
To make sure you are safe and warm.

Until the angels heard my prayer,
I searched the universe for someone to care,
Which made them send you to me,
To be together eternally.

I asked you if we'd ever part?
You said 'No' whilst giving me your heart,
What told me all this could be no lies,
Was when I saw the love in your eyes.

Beneath the twinkling glow of starlight,
I'll kiss and hold you oh so tight,
When I hear you utter a contented sigh,
Then I know I will love you till I die.

J Thorn

LOVE
(To my husband Tom)

When I found Tom I found love
It was like looking at the sky above
The clouds floating by the sky so blue
I knew that I was in love with you.

God was watching - it had to be done
Us not being two - but becoming one
God knew that we were meant to be
Together forever, just you and me.

I'll be yours forever.

Angela O'Rourke

CORN DOLLY

A stranger bled mid sheaves of corn,
Long ago in a Phygian field,
Cybele, mother of earth is pleased,
Corn spirit's caught for next year's yield.

The corn is cut, the stranger died,
His blood enriched the earth,
Corn spirit's held for another year,
Till harvest time's rebirth.

We plait and wind around around,
Long straws with heads and some without,
Nek dolly, drop dolly, Bridget's cross,
Do we wonder what we're about?

We are now weaving corn dollies
For a harvest festival show,
We never knew of that stranger
In a far field long ago.

Ivy Allpress

THE ADJECTIVE CELLAR

Nestling smugly twixt pepper and salt
The adjective cellar begins its assault
When carelessly picked by some epicure
Who sadly considers himself connoisseur

Once the poor dinner guest flips up the top
the words tumble out, they're awkward to stop
They bounce on the table and under the chairs
And yelling and screaming, they bound up the stairs

Normally nouns are wrapped up in chains
Tortured and bound and horribly maimed
now they're ecstatic about to be pleasured
as picturesque words stand up to be measured!

The vicar remarks on these halcyon days
Whilst Major Winstanley has Draconian ways
And poor Mrs Kinglsey's exordium chatter
Falls willy nilly on euphoric batter!

The twins are excited in ectopic manner
the cat's caught its tail in a Hashemite planner
the doctor is dissident, red in the face
flapping his hands with acrimonious grace

Sadly the dinner has come to a close
The adjective cellar is back in repose
The nouns are rebound, the adverbs placated
The vicar, the major, the doctor berated

But wasn't it fun to see how are language
Can blossom and bloom and happily languish
In even the narrowest pinch penny mind
When the fruits of the adjective cellar are vined!

Archie Wilson

JULIE'S SHIELD

I am serene, gentle and contemplative,
A seeker of truth, lover of beauty, art and wisdom.
A preserver of all nature's creatures
In old England and old Italy.
I now know how to define and beat my own bounds
Taking on neither fears nor attributes that are not necessarily my own
But walking through life with head held high.
A cycle of 2000 years has just perfectly closed.
A new cycle has begun with Alan.
Together we walk this pleasant land, side by side
World without end.

Julie Wakefield

A DIFFERENT VENUE

'Meet me' he said 'at the Old Castle Gate.'
He hope to be there round about eight.
Her heart beat quicker, romance in the air
She stood beside him, such a fine handsome pair.
His height was attractive, broad shoulders as well
A voice soft and tender, no wonder she fell
At their first meeting in that business hotel.

He led the group, after his presentation
The girls all agreed that he was a sensation
They wrote down their notes as they listed so keen
His eyes were so blue and his smile so serene
Then after lunch, as he chatted her up
She almost dropped her small white china cup
'Yes' she said eagerly, 'the castle at eight.'
Her eyes were so dreamy, as she thought of the date.

She went to 'The Castle' at the time appointed
He did not turn up, O she was disappointed
But she went to 'The Castle' down Taverners Lane
And waited, and waited, and waited in vain.
While the handsome young man at 'The Old Castle Gate'
Was soon forgetting his date who was late.
He met a fast brunette, so sweetly he kissed,
Another dumb female to add to his list!

Margaret Carter

THE GREEN HILL
(The Eye of Gloucester)

To climb the Eye of Gloucestershire
Whose gaze reigns over all.
From Cotswold edge and estuarine tide
These images belong to all . . .

To stir the mind from reflections as these . . .
The wind blows hill o'er vale.
The fields reply, chorusing the trees . . .
Singing its perpetual tale.

To sit upon this grassy knoll
I meander with clouds of night.
Dreaming of escaping this mortal coil
Soaring high, like the lark in flight.

But upon returning, speeding earthward bound
The words I feel are plain . . .
Though I must leave this hill with its lea below,
My soul will always remain.

Anthony Victor Bergonzi

FOR ALWAYS

A love which is strong, one that's lasted so long
Will never, ever say die, so believe me
If it did I would cry, as I do when I try
To forget you like this, feeling heartache and bliss
So it's pointless and I won't deceive you
There's still one final thought
I've uncovered and brought
To my friend I did constantly lean to
I'll stay close, you might need me
Even though you don't want me
And I'll love you as always, so deeply.

David Yule

YOU WILL NOT LIKE THESE WORLDS

I am twisted schism
finding ease
with comfort
of watching
pears fall
from cradle
broken
vowels fall
from my lip
juice of fruit
once bitten
drools down my chin
I am sin.

Ian Chambard

BARREL (FATHER'S FOOTSTEPS)

The day that we met
The first thing you said -
You were going to buy a barrel,
Line it with mattresses
And nail down the lid,
And then roll yourself, laughing,
Over Niagara's lips.

You were grateful, you said,
That you father was dead -
He thought you were going to be a bareback rider.
That had been bad enough,
But the barrel and lid
Would've killed him quicker
Than that frayed trapeze wire.

Robert Hammond

MAD COW AND FOOT AND MOUTH

Why are we shocked by the disease of foot and mouth?
That it has spread north, east, west and south.
Should we not know that nature has a way
Of making sure it has its day?

When we treat it with no respect,
We turn animals into cannibals, we get what we get
Animals should be grazing on luscious grass,
Out in the open fields, where their days should pass.

But we know that half of the year they are shut in sheds
Where they are crammed together head to head
Their food is little pellets of what?
Bits and pieces, of we know not.

It could be wheat, it could be grain
But it could also be animal brain.
If we do not take account of what we are doing
We can see what is happening, we are heading for ruin.

Can we, as humans, change the plan?
We have the knowledge,

For we are man!

Linda E Walker

WHY WAIT FOR ME?

Why wait for me?
I'm far too slow
I'm lagging far behind
Spirits ebbing low.
What is the point?
I'll never win
Shouldn't have entered this race.
You're being kind
I should be stronger
To have the courage to go on.

Why wait for me?
What is my worth?
I'm sinking further down
Crawling on the earth.
What is the point?
I'll never win
Shouldn't have entered this race.
You carry on
I'll be alright here
Go and do the best that you can.

Why wait for me?
I want you to go on,
Lost is all hope for me
But you must go on.
What is the point?
I'll never win
Shouldn't have entered this race
I'll cheer you on
You'll be my hero
The light and the strength to try again.

Amanda-Jane Tudor

ALL EXCELLING

Last night I dreamed that together we strolled
Through a riverside scene in the sunset's gold
With peace and beauty in all that we saw,
In tranquil contentment and, deeper, much more,
All was so perfect, the world was our own,
An exquisite stopped time shared by we, alone,
With fingers entwined, as our hearts were too,
I basked in the joy of just being with you,
We did not speak, what need be said
When the softest words may endanger a thread
As golden as the sunglow above?
How one *feels* how one *sees* when one is in love!

The vision was lost when I woke from that dream,
Gone were the river, the sunset's gleam,
No longer we walked there side by side
But the essence, the magic had not died,
Love's reassurance still coursed through my veins,
Its uplift, contentment, its joy still remains,
Like music it flows, a chorale in my blood,
'All is still well and safe, life still good.'
To be young and in love may be life's champagne
But to be older and yet to retain
That One, those feelings, against all the odds
Is surely the nectar of the gods?

Les Morris

SULAIMAN

God help me be a good boy
It's not easy for me you know
I cannot help being naughty
Wherever I may go

I have a little brother
And I love him very dear
But when I hug and kiss him
I pinch and cause him fear

I am taken to nice places
For me to sit and eat
I make a lot of noise and mess
And food lands upon my feet

I love to run from Uncle
He's not fast on his feet
When he cannot catch me
That makes my day complete

I am very fussy about my food
And want all that I can see
I like to chew and spit it out
It don't taste nice to me

Just love me as you find me
I am Sulaiman you see
Just a little time will pass
And a good boy I will be.

Mariam Ajaib

FINAL SUNSET

I watch transfixed, this wondrous sight of setting sun,
In all its beauty - gracious and graceful.
A perfect orb of serenity, of peace, of gentle strength.
A life-giving force, God sent.
In your presence, orange, pink and blue
All merge in clear, untroubled sky,
While thousands of golden jewels
Dance and dart upon the sea below.

Your golden frame, suspended by invisible threads,
Silently slips from spacious sky
And sinks into the ocean deep.
Your perfect form dissected by far-off horizon
As you melt into a watery grave.

You lighten our days and brighten our lives,
But all too soon, you are gone.

You go to shine on those in distant lands
But will you dawn once more upon our hemisphere?
To shine forth your radiance -
To continue on this ever moving journey -
This circle of life?

Will I ever see you again?
Will I wake to your brilliant rays
And feel your warmth upon my face?

Or was this my final sunset?

With my eyes I viewed it as my first
Whilst in my heart I cherish it as my last.

Stephanie Linney

GODREVY TOWANS

Sweet-smelling turf beneath my feet,
Bedecked with daisies and the golden buttercup.
A blue, blue sky above my head
Where white gulls wheel and cry
And skylarks soar and sing.
This is a lovely place to be,
Godrevy Towans, on the Cornish coast.

The wild Atlantic pounds the shore below;
Black-suited surfers ride the rolling waves;
Canoeists paddle out and back again;
And on the rock-strewn sands below the cliffs
Children run back and forth, shouting
And laughing, splashing in the sea.
Their parents lazing on the golden beach.

Godrevy lighthouse on the island, stands
Tall and silent, white walls gleaming in the sun.
To those who sail in St Ives Bay
It warns of black and jagged rocks
Beneath the waves; and when the winter storms
Unleash their fury on the Cornish coasts
Its friendly light guides seamen safely home.

Across the bay, St Ives lies sleeping in the midday sun,
Home to the painter, potter and the sculptor too.
Whilst around Godrevy Island, and the rocky coast,
Seals swim and fish, their dark heads bobbing,
Watching the people on the cliff and shore.
And in the evening when the sun goes down
The sky is shot with red and pink and gold.

Ann Linney

WE'RE ALL LIT UP IN MULLION (CORNWALL)

'Shall we have more lights this year?
How marvellous, what a great idea.'
So this bright thought was worked upon
And last year why, the village shone!
A great success there was no doubt
But this was only brought about
By helpers giving of their time
To raise the cash for lights so fine.
They didn't leave it there of course
But have been out again in force
To raise more money through *this* year
To give the village greater cheer.
So thanks to all who raised the lights
To make these *special* Christmas nights.

Paddy Jupp

THE METEORITE

The man in the moon was busy last night,
he was chasing after a rogue meteorite,
that was crashing to Earth, in full free flight.
        Let's hope it won't happen.

The galaxy was in disarray
the old Great Bear and the Milky Way
were agreed that all they do was pray.
        It won't happen.

The sun came up, but he'd nowhere to go,
it looked like the end of the world, what a terrible blow,
the clouds skimmed about, saying we told you so.
        But no one would listen.

The only one who could stop this disaster,
was the king of it all, the Lord and Master,
he would stick the pieces with spiritual plaster
        and rebuild the world.

Gerry Concah

I WISH I COULD

Two white beautiful unicorns
Galloping gently through the blue sea
Oh how wonderful it would be
If only I could ride upon thee.

If I could ride a unicorn
Across the shining blue sea
To a beautiful place of peace and tranquility
And the stars and moon shining down on me.

Oh yes I wish this could be
Wearing a pure white silk dress
That has been made especially
And beautifully only for me.

The unicorn rides no reins and saddle-free
Gloriously, calmly and spiritually free
How unique and intelligent the unicorn can be
Yes I wish I could be just like thee.

Joanne Mills

A Glimpse Behind The Scenes

Amidst the testing trials and worries of the world,
so often blinkered and preoccupied by daily life,
our inner being suffers and shrivels from neglect.
Driven relentlessly by financial need or greed
the racing years all but beat us to our goal,
while scattered family long since dried their tears
their patient love and caring eroded by the years.

Refreshed by moments spent in mindful meditation
our thoughts flow like a newborn mountain stream;
from rugged, barren, misty heights to sunlit leafy glade
where love and hope pervade the awakening spirit,
igniting ashen embers of the garbage-laden soul.
Rays of inspiration penetrate and pacify our thoughts,
on-line, connecting to the web of love and freedom,
actively communicating through the universal modem.

Unseen, a world awaits beyond our wildest expectations;
a garden of breathtaking beauty and spiritual serenity,
peace and tranquility, filled with happiness and joy
where thoughts become reality and love immortal.
Beyond the veil of death where precious life lives on
the spirits move amongst us like feathers on the breeze,
floating through our minds, drifting through our dreams,
guiding and protecting as they work behind the scenes.

J M Redfern-Hayes

FOR MUM

I love you more than words can say
I love you more each passing day
we've supported each other for many years
and I'll be there to talk you through your fears
I'll be there for you night and day
when you need me
you just need to say
whatever happens I'll be there for you
I'll support you in whatever you do
I just want to say how much I care
and if you want a shoulder to cry on
I will always be there
just remember how much I love you
and I'll be there always for you.

Linda Casey

THE OCEAN

Her digestive juices run,
Gurgling, frothing cappuccino
pseudopoedia in every direction,
Searching hungrily for fulfilment,
Then retracts, sometimes successfully,
Always searching, always moving,
Rolling, draining, crashing angrily,
Nibbling, gorging base of cliffs,
Pulling in sand, rocks,
And attacking again, with force,
Always hungry for power,
Using her enormous strength to dominate,
Destroy, digest and threaten.
As her demands are satisfied
And her system is full she settles,
relaxes, rolls gently, calmly,
Gulls rest on her soft counterpane,
Sun glistens on a still water.

Lynda Burton

FIRE AFIELD

Leaping tongues of thirsting flame
stubble burning once again.
Billowing clouds of acrid smoke
floating on the air to choke.

Charcoal carried on the wind
small black pieces drift and land.
Dust deposits all around
scorched earth searing cracking ground.

Now the hands have lost control
thick grey clouds rise in a pall.
Quickening wind has whipped in rage
as hedges catch in frightening blaze.

Insects scurry from the heat
and mice and voles with burning feet
in terror run towards the cool
searching for a water pool.

Songbirds fleeing from inferno
hedgerows smouldering in their wake.
Panic strikes upon the field
they try to make a quick firebreak.

But all the brush is tinder dry
and flames are leaping towards the sky
creeping crafty for the copse
where brittle pine trees and soft moss
await their threatening heated game
without a hint of fear or flame.

Elizabeth Cleveland

JUST PASSING

Pigtails, Poets, 'n' Ponytails,
Skipping out marble games,
Etched in the yard,
Together with our frantic mischievous faces,
Caught aging, simply aging,
Beside a wild crocus garden,
Kissed with drops,
In floods of laughter,
Time has run,
Said the mysterious sage,
From his pulpit chair,
Nursing wounds,
Touching gossamer wings
Where waters gather,
Catching the flag,
Waving, waving, noisily,
At Margret's passing, passing,
                    dutifully.

And now a nation celebrates a life,
As a Queen goes to join her Bertie.

Andrew Fry

MISSING YOU

I came away from Sussex
To this fair Devon town
The days of toil behind me
To try to settle down

But I miss the sea, the sound of waves
Alight with golden sun
Or calm and flat in sunrise
When the dark night is done

I miss the fog - the sea mist
And winter waves so strong
That wash the pebbles on the prom
And the seagull's haunting song

But I must admit in this fair town
I've found a little niche
There's neither job nor money
But the friendship scene is rich

Even here on Dartmoor grand
Things don't go without a hitch
It made my day when lots of sheep
Strayed on the cricket pitch!

The game was stopped, the umpires swore
When right behind them came
Some Dartmoor ponies charging down
And holding up the game!

The sun and shade, moor stark or soft
Fields, trees or steep ascent
With all this beauty round us here
Who could not be content

So while I'll miss you all a lot
In many different ways
The very fact of knowing you
Has much enriched my days

Enid Gill

A LITTLE VILLAGE

There is a little village,
tucked away and out of sight.
Hidden from the world's eye view
and all its troubled might.
The local folk are friendly,
and the pace of living slow.
People always have the time
to stop, and say hello.

The annual village ram roast
is the highlight of the year.
Humming with the visitors
that come from far and near.
The boys and girls play hoop-la,
the men do tug-o-war.
The locals sell their country fayre,
and bric-a-brac galore.

So, where is this little village,
that inspired me to write?
With its pretty cottage gardens,
and walls decked in white.
Where newborn lambs frolic
in the early morning sun.
And there always is a welcome?
Of course - it's Hemerdon.

Margaret Vincent

A Spot In The Eye Of The Poet

As we walked along the seafront
In the early afternoon sun
In the warmth of closest friendship
Hand in hand, with our thoughts as one

My blissful stroll and my reverie
Were suddenly broken awry
By a small black spot which appeared
On the right side of my right eye

Although it is quite small it comes
Into everything that I see
Even when I look in the mirror
I can see a spot upon me

Sweeping landscape or pretty face
It matters not, there is a blot
I have it there in front of me
In the picture, no matter what

The doctor at the hospital
Assures me it will go away
I will see the world as perfect
Wouldn't we all like to see that day

John M Spiers

MOONLIGHT QUEST

How I wonder who you are
The one of whom horses dream
Bare yard under moonlight
In the haylage a quick rat
Horses dreaming of you.

The wind burns your mind
It seemed no right way to bring
You here but the path was white
And you were expected.

You know they are here
Constellations flashing their
Deep quick life across the land.

Dream of impossible love chargers
To smuggle the gospel across
Sleeping land to troubled hearts.

Horse can trust,
Will show you the way,
Waits, dreaming, for you.

Gabriel Hummerstone

OF PLACE, OF PEACE, OF HOME

When, in church, I greet a dear friend
And to each other's needs attend,
With healing love our hearts do mend,
I have a sense of place, of peace, of home.

When in to work I daily go,
Joining the others as we row
In the river of tasks' smooth flow,
I have a sense of place, of peace, of home.

When looking in my partner's eyes
And lots of hugs erase my sighs,
Good feelings in our hearts arise,
I have a sense of place, of peace, of home.

When I recall what God has done,
As he sent his own precious son,
So in heaven we'll be as one,
I have a sense of place, of peace, of home.

Winifred Rickard

THAT DAY

A ghost ship lies off the
Cornish coast
It died in heavy seas, long ago
Some men were rescued
While others . . .
Misshapen rocks formed - since that
Fateful day
Some say
They are the dead men
While others
Don't like to say

On a strong stormy sea
Heavy with high winds and thunderstorms
You can still hear the men
Crying to be rescued
They howl like baying wolves

But when the sea is calm
Puffins perch
Unafraid
Upon misshapen forms

J M Stoles

PEACE

Alone up on a country hill
So quiet - so peaceful
No sound at first - but listen
The wind sighs in the long grass
Insects buzz, a lark sings its way upwards
Far away, the low of a cow, a cockerel crows
So many sounds on a quiet hill
But all bring peace.

Enid Broe

EXCESS BAGGAGE

'Leave all your mistakes
at the foot of my cross,
then come, and follow Me.
You don't need that weight,
still dragging you down;
It's time to stand up and be free.'

I start to protest -
'It doesn't seem fair, Lord,
to dump all this rubbish on You,'
and I feel embarrassed
for inside these bags
are my 'indiscretions' on view.

I turn from my Lord
to the cross where He died
to free me from suffering and shame,
then I let go my grip
on all I held dear
and my hands rise to worship His Name.

Mary Petrie

GRANDMA'S PLEA

Dry your tears don't cry for me
Life comes and goes it's got to be
Must live our lives the best we can
Woman, child and every man.

Comes a time when old we must be
We never believe it but wait and see
Special times we had when we look back
Joy and laughter dancing that's a fact.

Did we ever dream we would get old
Glasses, hearing aids, false teeth and feel cold
But here I am at last, safe, cosy and warm
Bring me my tea Jan, I'll weather the storm.
                    Goodnight with a kiss.

E Witt-Way

SNOW

I gaze out of my window
At the gently falling snow;
A million frozen raindrops
Alighting here below.

Transforming trees and rooftops
With a canopy of white;
Laying on the roadside
And freezing hard at night.

Causing driving hazards
That need the greatest care;
Making footpaths icy
For people ev'rywhere.

Piling where it's drifted
On the frozen ground;
Bringing out the children
To throw it all around.

Cutting off a village;
Blocking off a road.
It makes a pretty picture
But I wish it hadn't snowed.

Geoff Tullett

Two

Two met at a party
Shared a secret kiss
Two are parted in the week
But shared weekends are bliss!
Two fall more and more in love
Each and every day
Two decide that this time
Love is here to stay.
Two spend a weekend at the Lakes
Take trips as couples do
Two have excursions by the sea
And days at Bristol Zoo.
Two are getting married
A proposal made by phone
Two look forward to their wedding
And to finding their own home.
Two are smiling on their wedding day
In sailor suit and feather
Two are married, joined for life
Their love is sealed forever.
Two on a moped in Corfu
And swimming in the sea
Two tanned and laughing lovers
Those two are you and me.

Jody Louise Richardson

CHEDDAR

C heddar can be synonymous with cheese, caves and craftsmen's
                                                            skills
H owever it is sheltered from the wind by the Mendip Hills,
E arly strawberries ripen, row upon row, punnets soon overfill.
D aily, stone-filled lorries vibrate houses, nerves often jarred
D etonated from nearby quarries leaving scenery scarred
A s builders' demands grow so protest is met with disregard.
R ock climbers, helmeted, scale the limestone cliffs, these were
                                                          we know
G ouged out by nature's force in the Great Ice Age aeons ago
O ver the years people have strolled through the deep-cut gorge below.
R esidence of early man, caves now a tourist attraction
G aze at trees, playful trout, Mandarin ducks threaten disruption,
E ach visit to Cheddar ensures time for quiet reflection.

Mary Beale

MEMORY OF MY FATHER

I was a dining-room prisoner
Forced to perch on a sacrificial stool
A sea of newspaper at my feet
Set to capture my childish curls
Dreading the shark-like approach of the clippers
Rows of stainless steel teeth
Glinting serrated torturers.
Sitting ramrod-stiff
Streams of sweat saturated all my body
Like a terrified hostage
Or a rabbit mesmerized by headlights
Waiting for the executioner to strike
His fatherly hands gripping cut-price clippers
So much cheaper than paying hairdressing bills.

He cuffed my burning ears
Ensuring I kept absolutely still
Not moving freely as a mother's boy
The scissor rhythms knew no mercy
Mocking my captive's fear
A silent scream froze on my lips
It was a lesson in practical necessity.
Occasional drops of blood stained my shirt
A home haircut established dominance
Teaching me a suitable servitude
Never to question
Only bow the flesh-torn neck.

Christopher J Korta

Patchwork Heart

I'm trying to match up the pieces
Of this tattered old broken heart.
I'm not sure if I've got them all,
But at least I can make a start.

I will use invisible mending
So you won't see most of the seams.
It's really looking quite a mess,
I could use a medical team.

I'm trying to staunch the aching,
And I'm trying to stop the pain.
The hurt and the longing keep coming,
Those will need stitching up again.

I've had difficulty matching
The pieces, scattered far and wide.
One was lodged in a memory,
Another buried deep inside.

They found one in an old letter,
One was sent back from overseas.
A little bit was in a cold, grey room
Badly damaged by soul-deep pleas.

By hoping, loving and caring,
Why, it's almost looking like new.
Now there's just a small piece missing,
Is that the one I left with *you?*

Julia Whale

PRIMROSE HILL, SPRING MIST

It glowed sap-blue in the rain-mist,
   a full camel-hump
of a hill, like a waking ghost,
groved by hawthorns in leaf and wet
   as a baby's face.
The steep path suckled the sky's weight
and on reaching the top I breathed
   a rubbed-out skyline.
Yet in disguise that skyline seethed,
the screen of mist was mutely stained
   with towers, a whole
city was kept utter, contained
as a half-swallowed syllable.

Then I wandered the hill's purlieu,
   maples and hornbeams
twinkled and grasses, bleakly blue
in the year's veiled aubade, made bluff
   mounds against mudbeds.
And I'd caught spray from the year's wave
like a fever, so in the blocks
   of pastelled houses
below the hill, plaintive as smokes,
I saw a summer's blossom swell -
   pink, cream and sky-blue -
and in my descent from the hill
I rode the ebb of a meadow.

Chris White

SPRING 2002

Although sunny now for several days
There is a tinge of sadness in the haze
The spring which has arrived and blossom abounds
This year brings news of other sights and sounds

Bathed in sunshine and cooled by breeze
From far and wide they came, including overseas
People, to pay their respects and show this day
For order of a former time now sadly passed away.

Easter has gone along with thoughts of the Crucifixion
The procession to Calvary has been forgotten
For now we have witnessed the funeral of a beloved Queen
Who in our time won all hearts no matter where she'd been

The procession with all its pomp and majesty
gave credence to our thoughts for those whose loss it is
The eulogy, the hymns and prayers all meaningfully spoken
will be savoured and remembered when another spring has woken.

Yet many days are still to come when sunshine fills our hearts
and then perhaps we shall perceive that life has other starts
New chicks, new lambs, new growth and colour galore
life goes on and starts again just as it's done before.

So with the passing of the years as time goes rolling by
We shall remember this spring with sadness and with joy
because we have a Golden Jubilee to come,
another celebration, a cause for further fun.

Leonard Timbury

2002

Just like last year, Colin and I were
consuming herbal tea in bed.
In she came, dramatically,
with neon flashes of blue and red, and
green and gold, with plenty of big bangs. We viewed
these delights through the condensation,
upon the glass of our
bedroom window. Happy New Year!
We kissed and hugged! Welcome, welcome,
year 2002; you may not get the same
coverage and hype as the year 2000 did,
but that does not mean
much to my husband or
myself, who are not really into
silly, commercial hype.
The fireworks remind us both
of November,
and that is always such
a magical month.
2002, I hope that you
bring joy and
tranquility, and
I know to expect challenges and
many surprises. I
look forward, with hope and excitement,
to the year ahead.

Paula M Puddephatt

A STANDING OVATION FOR DENISE WRIGHT

The tall and slim Compere, announced
That Denise Wright was going to sing
There was a standing ovation
A real cause for celebration

When all was quiet, the curtain opened onto a pretty garden scene
Denise sat on a floral swing, just like a queen
With microphone in hand, she began to sing

When Denise Wright was only seven
People would say 'She's come from Heaven'
Big blue eyes, fair curly hair and a sunshine smile
A soprano voice that could travel half a mile

One day, when she was eight, she was not well
Her mother said 'Something's really wrong, I can tell.'
Her parents were faced with a terrible choice
With a soft and gentle voice
'It's meningitis' said Doctor Fry
She'd lose her legs or she would die!

It took months of struggle and despair
Lots of courage and tons of care
Much bravery and much talk
On artificial legs she began to walk

This is a story of courage, and it's true
I'm glad, I am the one, who's told it to you
Guess who is singing at the Kings tonight
The Indestructible Denise Wright!

Raymond Spiteri

MILLINERY OBSERVATIONS

The lampshade in green first attracted my eye
Then the beret, the colour of blueberry pie.
The bright yellow silk, with extended brim
And the mirage in mauve, with the too fussy trim.
Our visitor 'royal' wore a beehive in white
There, an apricot - crushed - what a terrible sight.
A boater in red, well you know what they say
Next door to the basket, in battleship-grey.
Just then it appeared, as it bobbed up the aisle
The blackest of hats in the old bucket style.
There on the side, for no reason at all
Was a large lump of white, in the shape of a ball.
With feathers that wafted between ball and hat
Now what I wondered was the point of all that?
Like a flash came the answer as to how it occurred
A snowball had landed, and brought down a bird.
I could never be tempted, not ever to wear
Any one of those hats to cover my hair.
High fashion and style are all well and good
But me, I rely on my duffel coat hood.

Kathleen H Allen

THE POTTING SHED

'All quiet in the potting shed'!
There is no rattle of tools and pots;
No 'clink and clump' that denotes
A gardener is at work - instead
The tools are hung - the boots by the door -
No footsteps crossing the paved floor!
See the garden through the open doorway,
Sunshine is on the terracotta centre pot,
Though shade is reaching the seat - it is hot!
Trees and bushes make a shady place to stay,
But, the cats have had enough of heat
And, no doubt, enjoyed their fill of meat!
The potting shed is quiet and cool
To sleep and 'snooze' in the afternoon lull;
The cat on the step thinks
    'Will they let *me* in as well?'
Rays of sun glance through the window;
Clothes upon the wall pegs show -
A lady gardener does her share -
Her ribboned straw hat is hanging there!
Planters hanging from a ledge above,
Fruit juice to refresh, in the window alcove;
Boxes and bins, quite tidily stacked,
And on the bench, a trug with flowers picked -
All clues considered - it might be said -
It could be a lady's potting shed!

Mildred E Wood

SHOEBOX MEMORIES

Away and beyond
The pendulum rises and falls
To the ticking and tocking
Of carious times

Sublime, moth-eaten
The parabola of destiny
Dry frail footnotes
Perceived through the glass

In the back of the cupboard
Revered shoebox shrine
Cardboard encased memories
How many sighs do they hold?

I try to guess as I decipher
The gleam beyond your so hooded eyes
There are valleys and mountains
Gracing your face

The sun used to reach
Those worn-down gullies
Now it's a memory
Because that's all you have.

Matt Keirle

DREAMING OF YOU

I saw your shadow
Though your face was unseen
I dream about you daily
What does it all mean
Is our story unfinished?
Are our minds combined?
In seeing the grand visage
Would the truth be unkind?

Warren W Brown

WHITE BONES

Feelings stir,
stomachs ache,
the nervous wait,
the shell fire burst,
the blinding flash
that sucks out life
to ruffled earth
as skull and bones

without a soul
without a name
some mother's son
her tears all spent.

When time expires
they'll march on still
toward another war
and ever closer
to familiar death!

Godfrey Dodds

CATS' CORNER

Cats' Corner
Hiss! Spit! Spat!
She did this
She did that.
Did you know?
Oh, my goodness me.
Paw! Scratch! Ouch!
Oh, just let it be.
Does it matter?
Who does what?
If it's not a crime,
It matters not a jot.
It's no hanging matter,
To what a person wears,
What money she has,
Or how she swears.
Cats' Corner
Miaow! Lick! Bite!
What did you say?
Did she really? When? Last night!
Miaow! Scratch! Paw!
Tell me more, more, more
Well, whatever else
Is Cats' Corner for?

Carol Ann Darling

BOXES

Oh how you like boxes to hide things away
Especially for pain, that won't go away
For those unmet needs, and unmet dreams
Unravel your heart, with its fragile seams
The box for ideas, some are old, some are new
You hold onto all, and give away few

There's the box for the present, the future, the past
Those wonderful moments, that never do last
The box for the jokes, and the times full of fun
Holds precious moments, spent with daughters and sons

For your work there's a box, that holds all your skills
Bursting with knowledge, it demands to be filled
Intellectual prowess, experience and care
Bestowed on your patients, you are gentle and fair
To hold a hand, and meet their needs
Giving them hope, like precious seed
This box-like cavern, continues to be
Your safety, your anchor, when you're all at sea

My favourite box, hides the boy and the man
Who doesn't believe, he is precious and can
Be loved for himself, and liked even more
In my heart he has written, a musical score
He's the man of my dreams, so gentle, he hides
From what he could be, his potential within
To climb out of his box, would be like a sin
My lover, my joy, my sadness, my pain
I'd relive each moment, again and again.

Irene Steele

COME THROUGH

Come through a hedge backwards
hair sticking up, like a hedgehog.

Sleeping a blustery blue winter
with gales whipping all around

the den where rest is sometimes
possible, though slow shaky it is,

glass rattling in its scruffy frame
setting the pointed teeth on edge.

Sometimes awake, in a grey fuzz
rubbing dry eyes, grip swallowing

razor-dry throat, heartbeats are
almost aching slow, living just, in

midst of wild, sharp, dangerous
storm that has bomb-blown up all

safety, spreading lost leaves, stone,
trees all lying around, adrift on a

sea of amber, lifeless garden rubbish.
Then a wild, very weak watery sun

arises, struggling fiercely through the
soft grey clouds encircling in the sky,

to make its first bright, daring, dance
as spring's flighted, gold messenger.

Catharine Hains

THE WEATHER MAN

The trees are incisive which,
Swing back and forth,
We have the shrubs that tell us it's sharp and
prickly,
Which are also known as the gorse.

We watch the trees to see them mellow, autumn
is with us as they shed their leaves,
The colours are distinctive, red, brown, and
yellow,

Around the country we see the animals to
graze,
But we don't give enough thought for the
farmers' praise,

The weather is changing, we are feeling the cold,
But this is Britain and we are bold.

David Burgin

DESERT HALT

Alone and rigidly still he sat proud by a rock
In the sand of the desert, empty even of trails.
I braked, the Landrover came to a stop a few feet away
Whilst I summoned the Arabic needed to ask if
I could help; food, drink or a lift . . . though God knows where to.
He had no requests, no curiosity; just a seeming
Contentment in this absolute, unbroken solitude.
I had intruded, and yet a selfish compassion
Demanded a gesture, a seal upon our encounter.
From my cigarette stock, a neat store of thank you's,
I tossed him a couple of packs. They fell within reach.
My aim was good and my conscience soothed but he did not
                                        look down.
He groped for them, breaking his stillness, chilling me to the bone.
He was blind.
I drove on.

Rex Baker

UNSPRUNG COIL

Pain and anguish filling my head,
Unreleased emotions of those now dead.
An unsprung coil that one day will explode,
How much longer can I bear this load?
Why can I not bare my soul -
And in so doing once more become whole?
To talk, to try to relate,
So hard when left so terribly late.

Yet, today it has to be
Time to set those demons free
As my legal friend addresses my past,
It seems the die is truly cast.
I transcend back a million years,
Relive despair - remembered fears and futile tears.
Yet, still unsprung the coil must stay,
Or how could I face another day?

M A Shipp Yule

FIRE AT HEAVEN'S GATE

A bright dawn rises in freedom world
Dark plans have been made through the night
The day breaks out and yields the cries of thousands
caused by hate from another way

Why are we so hated, this deed so ill-fated?
The amass caused from one man's mind
Scour the Earth, until we find
Remove his head, yet another one will grow
Meet force with force, and you will never know.

Go back when he was young, did he know right from wrong?
Does he know something we don't yet know?
Does he want the Earth's oil, so we can all grow?

So many rich, so many poor, can we meet in the middle
an open common door?
There is shock with bloodstained scars
Dark dust fills the skies, to dry cried eyes.

Has this been said, in the Book of Revelations,
is the yellow peril, the sand beneath the feet of a
poor man's nation?

If we are alone in the universe,
can we lower the killings and slow down the hearse?
But yet again we may go to war
our cause is liberty, it's what we're fighting for.
More blood, deaths and dust, just a lust for the Earth's crust.

In time out of the dark sky a big stone will be thrown
and the Earth could be reduced to the size of a grapefruit
to what was once known.
Two towers stood proud, but now to rubble:
we pray to our gods, as we know this means trouble.
May your god bless you.

Tom Samuels

WHAT A MAN

Every woman likes to be treated like a lady,
To be taken to nice places, dine out with candlelit dinners,
Have flowers and chocolates, gifts all the time,
We don't want a man to step out of line.
But this is real life, so what do we get?
None of all that, it's a dream in our head.
Instead we get a beer-swilling man,
Who wants sex whenever he can.
He watches football on telly with his feet up - so smelly,
He won't lift a finger in the house,
It's women's work, not a man's, not in this life.
I look back over this poem,
I'm so glad I am free,
I don't want a man to look down on me.
I'll stay single and happy until
The man of my dreams comes along,
But until that day I'll party right on.

Alison Hereford

THE TV

I have travelled the world, and seen it all
North, south, east and west, so much to explore
All the excitement of land, sea and sky
I ask myself, but for TV, is the reason why.

From my cosy armchair in front of the TV
What else can one wish for, and impatient to see
To feel the beckoning wind from swaying palm trees
And spray from the ocean of mountainous seas.

To taste the cuisine of countries near and far
Everything one can wish for when travelling by car
So much to learn from pictures, a revelation to see
Where would we be without our TV?

To see all the fashions and follow the sport
And hear all the news and weather report
To distinguish behaviour of countries with goodwill
Who make touring visitors so welcome to feel.

So where would we be without our TV
That shows all nations, the world to see?
No need to despair, as time passes by, with
A wealth of knowledge, and good health to get by.

C King

THE WRITTEN WORD

From the mind to a
Thought

From a thought to a
Letter

From a letter to a
Word

From a word to a
Sentence

From a sentence to
A paragraph

From a paragraph
To a page

From a page to a story

C Osborne

A LONESOME ONE

The weary old man
Stood outside the cottage door
His head bowed, he was alone,
He had always tried to please
His wife died from an ordinary disease,
The sea had taken his only son,
His loving son, the only one,
What had he done?
He was always ready to lend a hand,
But that was common in the land
Where he lived,
He felt he was a lonesome one
And still he wondered what he had done.
Lifting up his drooping head
He saw the ripple on the lake
The hill beyond was ablaze with sun
Thus revealed to him the Heavenly One
Who brought comfort to a lonesome one.

Phyll Ludgate

WISHFUL DREAMING

Being suspicious I followed where you led
Into a derelict building where all would fear to tread
I being curious to find out what you are about
Rumour and gossip tell me that I am always left out
Up a rickety staircase into a darkened room
I see a shape a female shape waiting in the gloom
He holds this form in his loving arms
She whimpers it's so touching I must admit
They have no cause to close the door
I witness all as they strip
Embracing as one this romance amongst the ruins
As they tumble and caress with all love ensuing
The floor beneath that engrossed pair who struggle and groan
Several storeys high as they of this passionate love intone

Eventually the floorboards give
And their bodies come tumbling down without a sound
Down, down their bodies hurtle they lay smashed on the ground
Just dust and rubble rises now all that faces me
As trembling with fear I move cautiously
My life is very dear

Reporting all to the authorities was this so right to do?
Immediately they send searches and I am proven true
There had been a great disturbance and the flooring had collapsed
No remains of any human bodies were found
Did I imagine all that?
Did I dream I followed you to that dilapidated place
Did I dream I saw you in a fond lover's embrace?
Perhaps it is my psyche or can I see the truth?
Or perhaps I am dreaming no one knows the proof.

R D Hiscoke

A DAY IN THE LIFE OF A CIGARETTE

Start out life in pristine pack
Shopgirl puts you neatly onto rack
Other packs go but they're not the same
Someone is asking for you by name
A five pound note - some change in return
Then off you go, ready to burn

Into a handbag filled with gear
Make up, a diary and other things here
Meet another pack all tattered and torn
Nearly empty and looking so forlorn
You are emergency stocks waiting in the wings
To run out a disaster - an unthinkable thing

Other pack's long gone - out of the bag
'Hey,' you hear her say, 'would you like a fag?'
Out you fly, your cellophane ripped
Upside down - out your innards tipped
Now you're open you can't stop the flow
Your contents seized, one by one they go

Into the mouth, hot burning light
Smoke inhaled to do what damage it might
Tar stays behind - into the gloom
Into the lungs - just enough room
Smoke blows out, smell stops over
Eau de Stale Cigarette odour

Back to the mouth, ash flicks to the floor
Freezing outside but No Smoking sign on the door
Smaller and smaller, now just a butt
Squashed in an ashtray until stubbed out
Or trod on the ground it doesn't matter
Soaked by the rain and made into litter

Carey Sellwood

IF ONLY . . .!

The Mardi Gras is over and from the distance comes,
The echo of brazen fanfares and insistent boastful drums,
Why did I join the watching throng, expectantly aglow
When I might have danced, or clowned and pranced
Within the passing show?
Why stood I, chained by doubts and fears,
Not following my heart,
For the Mardi Gras is over, and I never once took part!

The magic spell is broken, the vibrant rainbowed stream,
Has drifted into limbo like a half-forgotten dream,
But hope dies hard and whispers in the shadows of regret,
'The Mardi Grass *may* come next year!'
Perhaps I'll take part yet!

Betty Gardner

SOULS TAKE FLIGHT

O darling if my soul took flight
And met yours on a starry night
While we were sleeping separately
Then would you fall in love with me?

O if I write with words of fire
My sweetie could you be inspired
To say I set the real you free
And as you kiss me tenderly?

As sunshine on your sweet face pours
Please say forever I'll be yours
And I will say that I adore
Your lovely soul I'm yearning for

To be united, twinned with mine
So did you feel it's God's design?
That clever angels planned our fate
So with my pen I'll illustrate

A picture of the life we'll live
As people see the love we give
So we'll go walking I the street
While shining love on those we meet

With flags of tenderness unfurled
We'll start a love train for the world
We'll make this world-wide love increase
You'll have the Nobel Prize for peace

Phil McLynn

GHOSTS

When we are grown old
There is so much one can remember,
We have known so many, friend and foe alike,
View their shades that pass before the screen
Of our imagined vision;
Only to gently fade into oblivion
But they are not gone for ever
As from time to time we resurrect them in our thoughts.
As long as we survive, some will never pass away.
Many bring pleasant memories, others sad visions well forgot.
The best remind us of our hopeful youth
When all seemed happy to explore.
God was in his Heaven and all the world did well
But then sad disillusion followed
Shattering wistful memories of yesteryore
When cold experience revealed the light of common day.
Sooner or late I shall join these lonely shades.
How many in their thoughts will they myself remember?
I wonder, yes, I wonder.

Geoffrey F B Watts

UNTITLED

It's a while since I wrote a poem.
So I thought,
I will write one now.
The weather is rainy,
But in a way quite mild.
I'm actually sitting at home,
And from school I must pick up my child.

I've done my shopping.
I've done my cleaning
And everything is spick and span.
If it was an hour later than now,
To the school I nearly would have ran.

You see I love my children.
So much, so that I can say.
Whether it's raining or cloudy,
They always
Make my day, a sunny day.

M T Crawford

MISTER LATE

Can you tell me Johnny Ray
Why you're late for work every single day?
You have such a black
Way of seeing things Jack
I arrive early for the next morning I say!

Joan Wylde

ODYSSEY

The glittering starfields
dominate the realm of night
and are coldly remote
from humankind who live
on planet Earth
our tiny island in the sky

Yet it was from our world
that the space traveller
started his cosmic odyssey
a long, long quest
to discover the reason
for man's continuing existence
in our swirling galaxy

We do not understand the universe
which was thrust upon
its speeding voyage
by the creating explosion
of the mysterious big bang

The universe gathers speed
expanding into the vacuum
where nothing exists
no time, no space, no matter . . .
but the young cosmos makes nowhere
become somewhere
as part of the material universe

And now the space traveller
stands at the frontier
of the evolving universe
and becomes part of
the sacred cosmic soul.

Stephen Gyles

MY BEST FRIEND

I weeded it I dug it out
Filled it with peat, so plants would sprout
I fed it, nurtured it, watered it, did it with a rake,
Went off to buy some plants, my pretty trough to make
When I came back, plants all there to see
I sat pondering which one where whilst I drank my tea
I couldn't believe what I saw
My blackbird came down ,dug it all out and more
Then he looked at me as if to say
Don't think you can trick me I'll be back today.
Well, I planted my plants after putting peat neat
Then watched for him upon my garden seat
He came, he saw, he looked at me
I looked at him sternly, so he could see
But he summed it up, I loved him, he knew
And promptly dug them all out in my full view
Cross, no, a smile came in the end
For my blackbird you see is my friend.

Sue Starling

THE CAT

Each day the cat appears.
Her movements are lithe and graceful
And she looks beautiful, with glossy black hair,
A white bib and white-tipped ears and feet.
She settles at the foot of a wall,
Below a rose bush where the birds perch,
Or under a tree where they nest.
The birds are her prey.
She waits, then suddenly with tail waving, she pounces,
Causing death and destruction.
I try to chase her away, to no avail;
She just fixes her amber eyes on me,
Looks inscrutable, as though to say, 'I'm independent and free'.
I know that the ancient Egyptians revered cats,
Thought they symbolised Isis and Bast,
The goddesses of protection and fertility.
Regrettably I see this cat as a killing machine
And I frequently wonder why beauty is created,
To destroy or be destroyed.

Dorothy Springate

ANCHOR BOOKS
SUBMISSIONS INVITED
SOMETHING FOR EVERYONE

ANCHOR BOOKS GEN - Any subject, light-hearted clean fun, nothing unprintable please.

THE OPPOSITE SEX - Have your say on the opposite gender. Do they drive you mad or can we co-exist in harmony?

THE NATURAL WORLD - Are we destroying the world around us? What should we do to preserve the beauty and the future of our planet - you decide!

All poems no longer than 30 lines.
Always welcome! No fee!
Plus cash prizes to be won!

Mark your envelope (eg *The Natural World*)
And send to:
Anchor Books
Remus House, Coltsfoot Drive
Peterborough, PE2 9JX

OVER £10,000 IN POETRY PRIZES TO BE WON!

Send an SAE for details on our New Year 2002 competition!